DODD, MEAD WONDERS BOOKS include WONDERS OF:

Sigmund A. Lavine

WONDERS

Illustrated with photographs, drawings,

OF HIPPOS

and old prints

DODD, MEAD & COMPANY · NEW YORK

For Hilda and Bill who,
like the legendary hippo of the Ronga,
are "honorary grandparents"

ILLUSTRATIONS COURTESY OF: Author's collection, 8, 9, 10, 13, 27, 38, 63, 67, 69; Author's collection, Furne Print, 18; Author's collection, photo by Nicholas Krach, 12, 19, 21, 22, 24, 32, 33, 60; British Museum, 23; Honeck Studios, © 1980, 30; International Expeditions, 45, 48, 50, 51; Kazmar Porcelains, 26 *top*; Ira Kirschenbaum, *title page*, 34, 36, 39, 40, 49, 53, 58, 62, 71, 76; Betsy Lewin, from *Hip, Hippo, Hooray!* © 1982, published by Dodd, Mead & Company, 29; Library of Congress, 42; Lion Country Safari, Florida, 37, 46, 73; Museum of Fine Arts, Boston, Martha A. Whitcomb Fund, 1951, 25; Jane O'Regan, 17; SATOUR (South African Tourist Corporation), NYC, 11, 41, 55, 57; A La Vieille Russie, Inc., NYC, 26 *bottom*; Zoological Society of London, 6, 14, 61, 64, 75.

Distributed in Canada by McClelland and Stewart Limited, Toronto

Manufactured in the United States of America

1   2   3   4   5   6   7   8   9   10

Library of Congress Cataloging in Publication Data
Lavine, Sigmund A.
Wonders of hippos.
Includes index.
Summary: Traces the natural history and lore of the
common hippopotamus and the pygmy hippopotamus, two
species of plant-eating, amphibious, even-toed ungulates
that live in the muddy rivers of Africa.
1. Hippopotamus—Juvenile literature. [1. Hippopota-
mus. 2. Pygmy hippopotamus] I. Title.
QL737.U57L38   1983   599.73′4   83-14193
ISBN 0-396-08226-2

Contents

Common hippo (Hippopotamus amphibius) *and young*

1
Meet the Hippopotamus

"The broad-backed hippopotamus . . ."
—T. S. Eliot

Greek travelers visiting Africa in ancient times were amazed not only at the size of a beast they saw in rivers and lakes but also at its appearance. Convinced that such a huge and strange-looking creature had to be of supernatural origin, the Greeks called it the "Libyan monster."

In time, early naturalists from Athens and other Greek centers of learning journeyed to Africa, observed the ways of the so-called monster, and renamed it the "hippopotamus." The naturalists derived this name from the Greek *hippo* (horse) and *potamos* (river). However, although hippos lead amphibious lives, spending most of the day floating, they are not "river horses." The only thing horses and hippos have in common is that they are both hoofed animals.

Except for noting that the hippo spent most of its life in water, Greek naturalists displayed little interest in either its habits or its relationship to other animals. But the hippopotamus intrigued Roman scholars. Their curiosity about it led to a scientific study of the beast. As a result, the Romans correctly classified the hippo as a distant relative of the pig.

When Gesner published his famous work dealing with all the species of animals known to science in 1558, he not only incorrectly placed the hippopotamus among the horses but also pictured it eating a crocodile. Hippos are vegetarians—but crocodiles do feed on baby hippos.

However, as the centuries passed, the facts gathered during the Roman investigation into the life history and behavior of the hippopotamus were overlooked. For example, Konrad von Gesner, who was not only the leading zoologist of the sixteenth century but also an influence on scientific thinking for decades after his death, ignored the findings of the Romans. When Gesner compiled his monumental *Historia animalium*—the first attempt made to classify all forms of animal life—he placed the hippopotamus among the horses. Moreover, he called it *Equus fluviatilis*—Latin for river horse.

Anatomists—experts in the art of dissecting the various parts of animals and plants in order to determine their structure and function—have confirmed that the pig and the hippo are kin. Paleontologists have also found proof of this relationship in fossils. But the fossil record of the hippo's family tree has so many gaps that no specialist in fossil identification can trace it in detail. Nevertheless, it has been established that the ancestor of the hippo and all other hoofed mammals first appeared during the Paleocene epoch some seventy million years ago. Zoologists call its descendants "ungulates."

In time, two types of ungulates inhabited the Earth. One had an odd number of toes; the other was even toed. Although the odd-toed ungulates were the first to evolve, most did not prosper. The only odd-toed mammals that have survived to the present day are the rhinoceros, the tapir, and the equines—the ass, the horse, and the zebra.

On the other hand, the even-toed ungulates have flourished and comprise a vast herd of living species that has been divided into two categories. The first consists of the two-toed camels, cattle, goats, sheep, and other ruminants (cud-chewing animals) that have furnished food, clothing, and shelter to man since the early Stone Age. Swine and the hippopotamuses make up the second group, which is known to zoologists as the Suiformes. Not only do the Suiformes have simpler digestive systems than the ruminants but also they have four toes on each foot, as did the earliest known ancestor of the even-toed ungulates.

Compared to the majority of even-toed ungulates, the modern hippo is a newcomer. It developed in comparatively recent times. The pig-like anthracotheres—a group of animals that had adapted to living near water—were its immediate ancestors. The link between the amphibious anthracotheres and living hippos is forged by fossil remains unearthed in Africa where a giant anthracothere once roamed.

Eventually, hippos of various sizes—some far larger than

The early natural history from which these pictures of a hippopotamus and a tapir were taken states that they were related. This is not so.

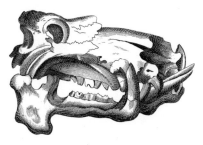

This old print was labeled: "Head of Fossil Hippopotamus found in Kirkdale Cave."

living species—flourished in all the warmer parts of the Old World. There is evidence that hippos were hunted with stone weapons by primitive man in places as far apart as China and central Europe. Skeletons of hippopotamuses are frequently exposed when foundations for new buildings are dug in London. Hippos grazed on the islands in the Mediterranean Sea in the distant past, while a species native to Madagascar and other islands off the east African coast became extinct in recent times. However, nothing has yet been found to indicate that any form of hippopotamus ever inhabited the New World.

Today, the hippopotamus is confined to Africa. Once common throughout that continent's tropical areas, it is presently unknown over much of its former range. Nevertheless, herds of hippos still can be seen in parts of central, southern, and eastern Africa.

There are two species of hippos living today. The common hippo, *Hippopotamus amphibius*, is much more numerous. It is a resident of estuaries, lakes, ponds, rivers, and springs. *Amphibius* competes with the huge Indian rhinoceros for the honor of being the second largest of all land animals after the elephant. But the common hippo's close kin, *Choeropsis liberiensis*, the species of hippopotamus found only in the jungles of Liberia, Sierra Leone, and parts of southern Nigeria in western Africa, is aptly called the pygmy hippo in common speech. Not only does *liberiensis* lack the bulk of its much larger relation but also it has a different shape.

While man has long been familiar with *amphibius*, he knows very little about the pygmy hippo. Discovered less than a century ago, *liberiensis* had been sought for nearly three hundred years. The search was hampered by conflicting reports concerning the appearance of an animal known to Africans as *nighwa* or *sen-ged*. This fabulous creature was variously described as a pygmy hippo, a small rhinoceros, or a giant pig. There was just as much confusion as to the mysterious beast's range. No one knew for sure whether it inhabited the deep jungle, mountainsides, or the water.

Because they lacked documented facts about the animal, many zoologists doubted its existence. But big game hunters and explorers looked for it. Most of them were convinced that their quarry was a large pig. After all, Olfert Dapper, a Dutch doctor

Herds of hippos can still be seen in Africa.

The zee-paert *was pictured in Olfert Dapper's account of his African travels published in 1668. Zoologists are still attempting to establish if the* zee-paert *was actually the pygmy hippopotamus.*

who visited Africa in 1668, had described in the record of his travels a monster pig that had "big sharp teeth with which it kills and rips open everything that crosses its path."

As the years passed, there was considerable speculation that Dapper's huge pig was actually a small hippo. Then, in the mid-nineteenth century, Joseph Leidy, curator of the Philadelphia Academy of Natural Sciences, made an announcement that was intended to disprove this theory. Leidy reported that he had identified two mammal skulls sent to him from Liberia as those of an animal that bridged the gap between hippos and pigs. Leidy named this intermediate form *Choeropsis liberiensis* —"animal from Liberia that looks like a pig"—and insisted it was extinct. When other authorities on both sides of the Atlantic examined the skulls, they disagreed. They maintained the bones were those of a hitherto unknown species of small hippopotamus that might still exist in parts of unexplored Africa.

The debate raged for years. It was seemingly ended in 1904 when an British Army officer stationed in Kenya shot a very large wild pig. He sent his trophy to London where zoologists found it to be a new species and named it "forest hog."

This old print shows a babirusa, a forest-dwelling wild pig of India. The giant forest hog of Africa is larger, weighing up to 300 pounds.

With the discovery of the forest hog—which lives throughout all of east and equatorial Africa—most scientists stopped arguing about the possible existence of a small hippo. The majority of them not only believed that the forest hog was the fabulous beast of native legend but also were willing to accept Leidy's classification of the Liberian skulls.

However, Lorenz Hagenbeck, a German animal dealer, was still convinced that a pygmy hippo lived in Africa. Therefore he persuaded Hans Schomburgk, one of his agents, to go to Liberia and look for it.

Schomburgk reached Liberia during the rainy season but began his search at once. He cheerfully endured the hardships encountered while trekking through unmapped jungle or while rowing miles in an open boat. But ridicule heaped on him by the Europeans he met at trading posts, as well as reports from

A pygmy hippopotamus, discovered at last in 1911—"a nice little animal."

natives that the animal he sought had been extinct for years, almost made him admit defeat and return to Germany. Then, on July 13, 1911, there, ". . . a bare fifty yards away, stood a creature no white man before had seen alive—a pigmy hippopotamus."

Realizing that the supposedly extinct dwarf was extremely rare, the jubilant Schomburgk did not shoot it. As a result, he was called a liar when he reported his discovery. Only Hagen-

14

beck believed him and sent him back to Liberia the following year.

On this expedition, Schomburgk saw several pygmy hippos. Determined to clear his reputation, he shot one on February 28, 1913, and carefully prepared its skin and skull for scientific examination. Meanwhile, another pygmy hippo was trapped in a camouflaged pit dug by Schomburgk's native guides. Although legend held that Dapper's giant pig was a fearful beast, this captive was extremely docile. Confident that he could take the pygmy hippo to Hagenbeck, Schomburgk, after much difficulty, arranged to have a cablegram sent to his sponsor. It read: "Caught a pigmy hippo—a nice little animal."

Eventually, Schomburgk secured four pygmy hippos. He transported them to Monrovia in large baskets carried by thirty-two bearers each. Upon reaching Monrovia, he transferred the animals to a vessel sailing to Germany.

As indicated, we know little more about *liberiensis'* life in the wild than we did over half a century ago. But the pygmy hippo's behavior in captivity is well documented. All who have observed its ways in zoos and wild animal parks agree that it is, indeed, "a nice little animal."

2
Lore of the Hippopotamus

"It is a strange beast that hath neither head or tail."
—Draxe

The ancient Egyptians, like many other peoples, believed that the forces of goodness and light waged constant war against the forces of evil and darkness. According to Egyptian religion, the leading figures in this bitter struggle were Horus, a benevolent sun god, and Set, the personification of wickedness. The complete record of the conflict between these two would fill several books the size of this one.

Tradition maintains that during the last fight between Set and Horus, Set, a master of magic, turned himself into a red hippopotamus. At first it appeared that the huge beast's great strength and long sharp teeth would make Set victorious. But after a long and bloody battle—so the story goes—Horus managed to slay the hippo with his bare hands.

Egyptian priests told the tale of Horus and Set to their followers in order to convince them that, in time, good always triumphs over evil. This lesson was enforced by a religious festival. Each year a celebration of Horus' victory was held at his temple at Edfu in Upper Egypt. During the ceremonies, a

16

Epet, the hippopotamus goddess of Egypt, was depicted in many forms by ancient artists. But whether shown with a crocodile on her back or wearing sacred symbols, Epet was always represented as having the feet of a lion.

group of priests poled a raft to the center of the temple's sacred lake. Then they cut to bits a large cake baked in the shape of a hippopotamus.

Despite its close association with Set, Egyptians did not consider the hippo a totally evil animal. Actually, they had mixed feelings about it. In some parts of the country it was held to be an abomination. Elsewhere it was revered. The Egyptian attitude toward the hippo is seen in the attributes bestowed on the goddess Epet, who also bears several other names. This powerful deity was always depicted—with minor variations—as a hippopotamus with lion's feet.

Originally a local deity whose worship spread rapidly throughout Egypt, Epet was both loved and feared. Considered a malevolent, dagger-wielding creature of vengeance on one hand, she was held to be an exceptionally kind and benevolent deity on the other.

Besides being thought to help the sun rise every morning and set each night, the hippopotamus-goddess supposedly prevented sickness. Epet was particularly beloved by the middle class, who named their children after her, decorated her statues, and wore amulets fashioned in her image.

17

Printed over one hundred years ago, this picture depicts a hippopotamus on the banks of the Nile. Note the Egyptian temple on the far side of the river.

One of the reasons Epet was so highly regarded is that she was said to guide souls during their hazardous journey to the Underworld. There are several references to Epet in the *Book of the Dead*. This manual, which was placed in the tomb along with the deceased, contains exorcisms and prayers to the various deities and spirits associated with death.

Powerful as Epet was, neither she nor any of her fellow deities could prevent the Romans from conquering Egypt. The invaders celebrated by erecting temples honoring their own gods and goddesses throughout the Nile valley. In time, these Roman divinities acquired the attributes of the Egyptian supernatural beings they had replaced. For example, Minerva, the Roman goddess of wisdom, inherited several of Epet's abilities. But the huge statue of a hippo that stood before Minerva's temple in the city of Sais did not celebrate the hippopotamus-goddess' good deeds. According to an ancient chronicle, the statue denoted " . . . murder, imprudence, violence, and injustice."

18

Today, clans belonging to many African tribes venerate the hippopotamus and employ it as their totem. Because the hippo is a large and strong beast, these groups originally claimed relationship with it in hopes that the powerful animal would protect them in return. For example, the Skai of Cameroon claim that hippos will overturn the canoes of any enemies that may come near a Skai village.

The Skai and other tribes living along the course of the Niger River are convinced that the soul of each member of a hippo clan is bound up with the soul of a particular hippopotamus. If that beast is wounded or killed, its human counterpart will suffer the same fate. This is why members of the hippo clan— who are forbidden to eat hippopotamus flesh—always warn the hippos when their fellow villagers plan a hunt.

Among the Hottentots of South Africa, the hippo clan is not only barred from eating hippo meat but also is prohibited from saying the animal's name. On the other hand, Basuto tribesmen who live nearby employ their word for hippopotamus as a ceremonial greeting. In other tribes, fetishes fashioned in the form of hippos play an important part in religious rites.

Artisans have fashioned hippos from many different materials since prehistoric times. The one shown here was carved from a piece of rare wood by a native craftsman in Kenya. Fetishes were fashioned in the form of hippos in some tribes.

19

Because the Mbedzi of Zimbabwe consider all animals that dwell in bodies of water sacred, they hold the hippo in great esteem. However, the Mbedzi do not have the same relationship with the hippopotamus as do the Raganda, the tribes for which the country of Uganda is named. Tradition holds that the members of the Raganda hippo clan are the descendants of a supernatural tortoise that was magically transformed into a hippopotamus when the world was young.

The hippopotamus is one of the few animals that have been ignored by the credulous. To be sure, there are a few superstitions concerning the hippo current in Africa but they have not been adopted elsewhere. This is because these beliefs arise from religious practices and the conviction of primitive man that he had to appease the spirits of the animals he killed.

Primitive African tribesmen are convinced the hippo has a soul that survives the death of the body and either wanders about as a spirit or is born again in animal form. Thus, when no laws protected the hippo and natives depended upon it for meat, hunters appeased their victim by engaging in elaborate ceremonies. This was because they feared that the spirit of the dead animal as well as all living hippos would seek revenge.

The ritual performed by the Ajumba of West Africa was typical of these rites. When a hunter of this tribe killed a hippopotamus, he decapitated it and removed the internal organs. Then, taking off his clothes, the hunter entered the rib cavity, knelt down, and washed his body with the animal's blood. At the same time, the hunter prayed to the hippo's soul, begging forgiveness and petitioning it not to ask a living hippopotamus to punish him by overturning his canoe.

Equally elaborate rites took place before the start of a hunt to insure its success. Before going to a hippo pool, Ubana hunters scattered flour on the ground, rubbed their spearheads in it, and beseeched the spirits to allow them to make a kill. If their prayers were answered, the grateful hunters ceremonially cooked the hippo's heart and liver and ate them while offering thanks to the supernatural beings for their help.

Until the huge herds of hippos that live along the shores of Lake Edward were granted protection, they were a sure source of meat to the Bakitara. Custom decreed that members of this tribe could only seek hippos between midnight and four o'clock or in the morning. Moreover, if the hunters encountered a frog or a woman on their way to the lake, they were required to return home.

Credulous Africans maintain that hippos often inform humans of future dangers. The animals do this, so it is said, in repayment for the warnings given them before game laws protected the great beasts. Incidentally, hunters never worried for fear they would kill a hippo clansman who had temporarily assumed the form of a hippopotamus. The human-turned-animal could be counted on to identify himself by raising one of his forelegs.

While early explorers laughed at the superstitions Africans had about the hippopotamus, Europeans are responsible for two outlandish beliefs about the animal. One is that newborn hippos viciously eat their fathers. The second is just as fanciful. It contends that hippos vomit fire. This superstition very likely

All of the illustrations in Charles Catton's Thirty-Six Animals, *published in London in 1825, were supposedly drawn from life. However, Catton never saw a living hippo. Note the teeth, about which Europeans spun outlandish stories.*

stems from the discovery that when one of the hippo's extremely hard teeth is struck with a piece of iron, it will "spark."

In ancient times hippo teeth were thought to have great magical powers. Not only were amulets fashioned from them but also wands. When placed near the bed of the owner, these wands were credited with providing protection from all types of harmful creatures. Both the material from which the wand was made and the representations of minor gods incised on it were believed to have remarkable properties that could be invoked by rubbing the wand.

Not only amuletic wands made from hippo tusks were thought to have curative powers. Other parts of the animal's body were employed by African shamen during their healing rites. But early European doctors who compounded the blood, bones, skins, flesh, and organs of animals in their "prescriptions" ignored the hippopotamus, although they were familiar with it. As early as 29 B.C., the Roman emperor Octavius Augustus displayed a hippo in his zoo.

Octavius' hippo was fortunate. All the other hippos sent from Egypt to Rome were pitted against lions and crocodiles in the "games" that delighted the Roman mob. In order to insure that

Many 19th-century delineations of the hippo emphasized the teeth.

Made for the wife of an Egyptian noble some four thousand years ago, this wand of hippopotamus ivory, incised with the figures of gods, supposedly protected its owner from harmful creatures.

these hippos would fight, their keepers forced intoxicants down their throats to excite them.

While hippos were being slaughtered in the arena, the famous Roman naturalist Pliny the Elder was suggesting that the animals could teach physicians how to control the weight of their patients. In the fifteenth century, Leonardo da Vinci, the famous Italian painter who had an avid interest in natural history, suggested the same thing to the doctors of his day. Da Vinci, like Pliny, detailed how a hippo loses weight. "When it feels itself becoming overloaded," wrote da Vinci, "it looks about for thorns or where there are the fragments of split canes, and there it rubs a vein so hard as to burst it open, and then having allowed as much blood to flow as may be necessary, it besmears itself with mud and so plasters up the wound."

Although the barber-surgeons of yesteryear did "bleed" those with high fevers in the belief that the technique would reduce their temperatures, doctors have never employed bloodletting to control weight as Pliny and da Vinci advised.

Some five thousand years ago, an unknown artist scratched

Tomb painting from Thebes depicts Egyptian nobleman spearing a hippo. The three ropes in the hunter's hand indicate he has wounded it three times and is pulling it to the surface while an attendant uses a lasso. The nobleman is preparing to throw a fourth spear. Note fish and baby hippo at bottom of picture and birds rising from reeds.

a hippopotamus twelve feet long on the face of a cliff at the edge of the Sahara Desert. Similar deeply incised engravings of hippos have been found in Algeria and in Libya. Archaeologists —students of past human life and activities—theorize that all these representations of hippos have religious significance.

On the other hand, it is obvious that the Egyptian artists who decorated the ruins at Thebes were not concerned with the supposed divinity of the hippo—the paintings depict nobles hunting it. Yet the close association of Epet and the hippopotamus inspired other artisans to feature the hippopotamus goddess in pictures and statuary. Still other craftsmen fashioned hippo-shaped pins, brooches, and ornaments from precious metals and ivory. But the most popular of all their creations were pottery hippos with a rich blue glaze. These were the favorite toys of the children of both Pharaoh and peasant.

Meanwhile, throughout Africa, small objects were being made

from the teeth of the hippopotamus. While the carvers displayed considerable skill, they were not the equals of the Phoenicians, the ancient world's principal workers of ivory. Despite the fact that hippo ivory is extremely hard and more finely grained than elephant ivory, the Phoenicians transformed it into exquisite works of art.

It is doubtful that George Washington found any beauty in hippo ivory. Washington, like many other individuals of his time, was fitted with a set of false teeth made of hippo ivory. The teeth were most uncomfortable. Seeking relief, Washington asked Paul Revere to fashion him a set from another material.

Although no longer used in the manufacture of dentures, hippo ivory is presently employed to make cane and umbrella handles. Because of conservation measures, the only teeth that reach the market are those taken from dead hippos. As a result, hippo ivory is quite expensive.

Even more costly are masks representing hippos or masks that combine the animal's features with those of humans. Formerly widely used in dances and other tribal rituals, these face coverings have fallen into disuse as old customs give way to the

Although the Egyptians hunted the hippopotamus, they treated it with affection and humor when fashioning toys for children. This pottery hippo was made between 2150–1785 B.C. by an unkown craftsman.

25

From 1870 to 1914, the famous firm of Faberge, goldsmiths and jewelers to the Imperial Court of Russia, created exquisite representations of animals. The hippopotamus to the right is carved from hardstone and has gems for eyes.

Modern craftsmen, like the artisans of ancient times, fashion hippos from a wide range of materials. The one above, from the world-famous Kazmar Studio, is made of porcelain.

demands of civilization. Prized by collectors and museums, hippo masks are primitive art at its best.

For some reason—perhaps because it is so ugly—the hippopotamus has not inspired masters of the brush. However, Sir Edwin Landseer, the famous English animal painter, was fascinated by the young hippo exhibited in the London zoo in 1850. The animal also enthralled Queen Victoria, who wrote in her diary on July 18, 1850, "We went . . . straight to the house where the hippopotamus is kept." Whether Victoria visited the hippo before or after she added the sketches Landseer made of it to the royal art collection is unknown.

Today, craftsmen fashion hippos from materials ranging from wood to precious stones. "Yawning" hippos serve as ashtrays and toothbrush holders, metal hippos are used as doorstops, and tiny tots go to sleep clutching down-filled, plushy hippopotamuses.

According to the Bantu, the first hippopotamus was an unhappy animal. One day while the hippo was sulking—so the tale

It is extremely doubtful that the artist who drew this picture for a weekly newspaper published nearly a century and a half ago ever saw a live hippopotamus. Nevertheless, his delineation is remarkably accurate. Note the "yawning" hippo on the right, and the birds in the background.

is told—an egret informed him that she admired him greatly. This made the hippo so happy that he stopped sulking and invited the egret to stand on his back whenever he was floating. The bird accepted the offer and, from that day to this, egrets and hippos have been close companions.

This folktale explaining why the so-called tick birds associate with hippos is unusual. In most folk stories, the hippo is held up to ridicule by detailing how various small animals outwit it. However, a Ronga story does credit the hippo with being wise and kind. According to the Ronga, somewhere in Africa there is a hippo that acts like a benevolent fairy godfather—it rescues lost and abandoned children. Asking no reward, the hippo returns the lost youngsters to their parents and finds homes for those that have been abandoned.

As indicated, ancient naturalists wrote extensively about the hippopotamus. However, their findings were more fanciful than factual. Pliny assured his readers that hippos are so wise that they walk backward to confuse hunters who pursue them. While we know that Pliny was mistaken, scholars still debate whether or not behemoth described in the Book of Job in the Old Testament was a hippopotamus. But the experts agree that the compilers of the first Armenian version of the Bible erred in translating the word *Nhanga* (evil spirit) as hippopotamus.

While the hippo appears in the works of Shakespeare, Kipling, and Lewis Carroll, generally speaking it has been ignored by writers of prose. Conversely, poets, particularly those who write humorous verse, have made good use of the hippo. Among the modern poets who have treated the hippopotamus in amusing fashion are Hilaire Belloc, T. S. Eliot, Oliver Herford, Samuel Hoffenstein, Arthur Guiterman, and Odgen Nash.

Nor have authors of children's books overlooked the hippo. No

Hippos are popular characters in children's books. This one is from Hip, Hippo, Hooray! *by Betsy Lewin.*

picture books are more delightful than those dealing with the adventures of a hippopotamus named Veronica as recounted by Roger Duvoisin. Then there are, among others, Bernard Waber's charming *You Look Ridiculous Said the Rhinoceros to the Hippopotamus* which teaches a sugar-coated lesson in tolerance, Nancy Winslow Parker's unusual story about a super pet sent with *Love From Uncle Clyde*, and Betsy Lewin's rollicking *Hip, Hippo, Hooray!*

Although "hippo" was employed as a slang term for automobile in the mid-1920's, the hippopotamus has made little impact on common speech. However, rude individuals are apt to say that an overweight person is "fat as a hippo."

The ungainly hippo is no more popular with composers than with the creators of slang. But most teenagers who have attended summer camp know the song describing the troubles Noah had loading the Ark. According to this song, when the animals were coming in " . . . four by four, the great big hippo got stuck in the door."

There is something comical about the idea of a hippo being

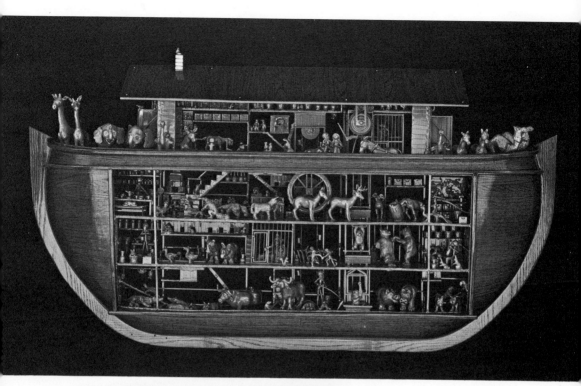

This Noah's Ark carries a cargo of animals sculptured by a master craftsman. Can you find the hippo? (See inset.)

so huge that it became caught in the door of the Ark. But far more amusing is watching the troupe of tutu-wearing hippos attempt intricate ballet steps to Ponchielli's "Dance of the Hours" in Walt Disney's famous cartoon *Fantasia*.

3
Physical Characteristics

"He is ugly beyond expression."
—Montagu

At first glance the pygmy hippopotamus closely resembles the common hippo. However, while *liberiensis* appears to be a smaller version of its larger kin, the two differ slightly. Special attention is directed to these dissimilarities on the pages that follow. Otherwise, it should be understood that the physical characteristic being discussed is identical in both species.

If a contest were held to choose the ugliest living beast, the common hippo would be leading contender for that dubious honor. Few animals are more unprepossessing—the ponderous hippo gives the impression of unmanageable bulk. Indeed, Robert Ardrey, world-famous authority on animal behavior, insists that the common hippopotamus "is the most unattractive creature that land or water supports."

Thomas Macauley would have approved of Ardrey's opinion of the hippo. In 1850, the famous British historian visited the London Zoo where the first living hippopotamus to reach

The tropical vegetation in the background and the head of the submerged hippo are products of the artist's imagination, but the hippopotamus pictured is the one exhibited in London in 1850. It was the first live member of its species to reach Europe since Roman times.

England was being exhibited. Upon returning home, Macauley wrote to a friend, "I have seen the hippopotamus both asleep and awake, and I can assure you that asleep or awake, he is the ugliest of the works of God."

There is no doubt that *amphibius* lacks a single eye-pleasing physical feature. Not only does its huge bulk make it appear ungainly but also the common hippo has an appalling shape when viewed from the side. This is because the long, massive, barrel-like body is set on such short legs that the belly is low enough to scrape along the ground. Moreover, although the common hippo's neck has considerable girth, it looks far too weak to support the monstrous head.

Size

While common hippos with bodies up to fourteen feet in length are not unusual, the average fully grown male (bull) of the species is 11½ feet long from nose to tail. Females (cows) are not as long. Both sexes stand about 4½ feet tall at the shoulder when mature.

Generally speaking, male common hippos weigh between 1½ and 2½ tons, cows a few hundred pounds less. However, larger individuals are known, some weighing as much as four tons. The big game hunters who visited Africa in the mid-nineteenth century undoubtedly shot hippos that were even heavier. In modern times, the largest recorded hippopotamus weighed 8,960 pounds.

The pygmy hippopotamus is more lightly built than its huge kin. It stands between three and four feet tall at the shoulder, has

The artist who drew this picture frankly admitted he had never seen a hippopotamus, but he captured its appalling shape in this sidewise view.

33

A common hippo photographed recently in Africa

a body length of approximately five feet, and rarely weighs over 500 pounds.

While common hippos have barrel-like bodies, those of pygmy hippos are torpedo shaped. Moreover, not only is the smaller species' body much shorter but also the rump has a distinct backward slope. Thus, *liberiensis* has a more piglike appearance than the common hippo.

Legs

Both hippos have legs that are structurally similar to those of pigs, but the legs of the pygmy hippo are relatively longer than those of *amphibius*. There is also a slight difference in the feet— those of pygmy hippos are less compact.

The stubby legs of the common hippo look far too weak to support such an enormous and heavy body, despite their pillar-like construction. But *amphibius'* limbs can carry a tremendous load as well as clamber up rocky riverbanks and run relatively fast over open ground. Further, the common hippo can move quickly through water either by swimming or by loping along the bottom.

Hippos' feet are the most primitive type found in the even-toed ungulates. All four toes of each foot rest flat on the ground, each toe being covered with a round, black, nail-like hoof. Hippos, unlike the majority of even-toed animals, do not walk on the tips of the two middle toes. They distribute their weight evenly among all four toes, which are loosely bound together by an elastic fibrous tissue and overlaid with a protective cushion of hardened skin.

Head

Usually all that can be seen of a floating common hippo is its partially submerged head, which may be 3½ feet in length and weigh over half a ton. It is just as well that all of the face does not show. There is little beauty in the great rounded muzzle, slitlike nostrils, and heavy eyelids that jut out to protect beady and protruding eyes on knobby pedestals. When a hippo is under water, the cavernous mouth is completely sealed by the large upper lip. But when on land, common hippos can open their mouths so wide that there is a four-foot gap between the upper and lower jaws, revealing the animals' formidable teeth. The awesome creatures seen in nightmares are less frightening than a yawning hippo!

There are minor differences in the dentation of the two species. Pygmy hippos have only a single pair of incisors (cutting teeth) in the lower jaw, while the common hippo has two pairs. In both species the incisors and the canines (tearing teeth) are tusklike and grow continuously. The two inner canines, which are kept razor sharp by rubbing against the upper teeth, are enormous.

With only its eyes, ears, nostrils, and the top of its head above water, a wary hippo emerges and watches the photographer.

Roaring defiance, a bull hippopotamus yawns to intimidate trespassers and warn rivals to stay away. Note the huge incisor.

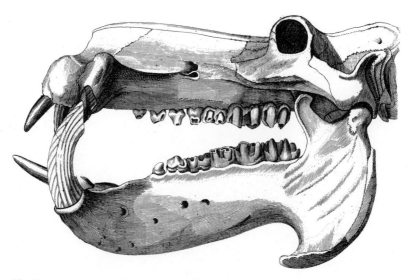

Skull of a common hippopotamus shows the teeth.

However, less than half their length protrudes from the gum. Common hippo bulls often have canines over three feet long that weigh as much as seven pounds and are ten inches in circumference.

In addition to powerful canines capable of crushing a crocodile's plated hide or biting a man in half, and incisors strong enough to dig salt and other minerals out of the ground, hippos have numerous molars. These teeth are adapted for chewing vegetation, which is pulled up with the lower lip and front teeth and ground with the back teeth.

When the molars wear down, a hippo cannot chew, and it dies from starvation. Thus, the longevity of an individual depends, to a great extent, upon the condition of its teeth. Hippos *may* reach an age of forty-five years in the wild but zoologists estimate that the average expectation of life is only ten years.

Some hippos die of hunger even though their molars are in perfect condition. These individuals develop an abnormal tooth in the lower jaw that grows in such a way as not to be ground down by the opposing tooth. If this malformed tooth pierces the roof of the mouth or severely tears the upper jaw, the hippo will be unable to eat.

Sensory Organs

Because hippos spend so much time in the water it is logical to assume that their eyes are adapted for aquatic vision. However, neither the bulbous, red-rimmed eyes rising like periscopes from the top of the common hippo's head nor the large round eyes on the sides of the head of the pygmy hippo have such a modification.

Not only are hippos unable to see clearly underwater but also they do not see very well on land. Research has revealed that both species are nearsighted and depend more on their ears than

Note the bulbous eyes on this snoozing common hippo. It seems to be smiling in its sleep.

Eyes and ears show that something is disturbing these common hippos.

on their eyes to detect possible danger. A single shout will awaken a herd of hippos sleeping on a sandbank and make them stampede to the safety of water.

Compared to the size of the head, the hippo's round ears are tiny. Positioned high and far back on the head, they fold when the animal dives. This partially blocks the opening. Then, as the colossal head rises out of the water, both ears wigwag back and forth independently of one another, which clears them.

It is far easier to determine the keenness of *amphibius'* hearing than it is to establish the acuity of its sense of smell. Nevertheless, zoologists are convinced that the common hippo's sense of smell is well developed. This belief is based on the knowledge that when common hippos raid plantations they ignore the green fruit but feast on what is ripe. Such fruit, zoologists point out, has a distinct aroma.

The nostrils of both species of hippo are located at the top of the snout. While the common hippo's nostrils are slitlike, the widely separated nostrils of the pygmy hippo are almost circular. Both types of nostrils are automatically closed by muscular valves whenever the head is submerged. As the head is lifted out of the water, the nostrils open with a loud snort and eject a fine spray.

Skin

Except for scanty eyelashes and sparse bristles on the muzzle, inside the ears, and at the tip of the short tail, hippos appear hairless. However, there are extremely short hairs on most of the body.

Covered with a network of wrinkles and deeply folded at the neck and chest, a hippo's rough, warted skin is very tough and quite thick. This is particularly true of the common hippo's skin

When a hippo swims, only its broad back, small ears, periscope-like eyes, and nostrils are above water. Note the roughness of the skin on the back of this hippo.

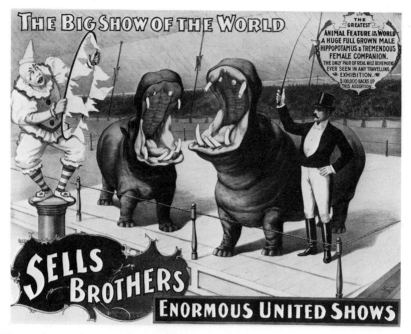

Circus fans of yesteryear flocked to the Big Top to see the "blood-sweating behemoth from the wilds of Africa." However, the sights depicted on colorful circus posters were rarely duplicated in any ring.

which is two inches thick where exposed to a rival's attack. According to Bernhard Grzimek, internationally famous zoologist and conservationist, it takes at least six years to tan a common hippo's hide properly. When tanned, the skin is as hard as cement and " . . . it is not surprising that it can be used for cutting diamonds."

Pygmy hippos' skins are a slaty green-black above, somewhat grayish on the sides, and grayish-white to yellow-green on the underparts. The "leather coats" of common hippos come in a variety of browns. Some are a slaty copper-brown shading to light brown above and purplish below. Others are a slaty copper-brown shading from very dark above to pink on the underparts, face, and neck. Still others range from dark leather-brown to bluish-gray and may be more or less spotted. The most striking coloration is that of the rare albino. Countless blood vessels just beneath the surface of the skin give it a brilliant pink cast, although the skin itself lacks pigmentation.

Despite travelers' tall tales, ancient belief, and the garish circus posters of yesteryear, hippos do not sweat blood. Indeed, hippos lack sweat glands. But glands under the skin do exude droplets of a brownish oil that takes on a reddish hue in bright light. This secretion keeps the skin pliable and prevents it from drying out in the hot tropical sun.

A number of zoologists believe that the so-called blood sweat has curative powers. It well may be so. Although hippos with severe wounds do bathe in filthy pools and wallows, their injuries heal quickly and cleanly.

Voice

Except for snorting when clearing their nostrils after a dive, hippos may not make a sound for hours. But they are not silent creatures. With voices that range from deep bass to screeching soprano, they are capable of producing a number of cries and calls.

The repertoire of the hippo is blatant and vociferous. Hippos bellow and roar when angry, scream with pain, neigh like a horse when excited, growl when provoked, squeal and shriek while fighting, and utter low grunts when traveling over rough ground.

Actually, the only time a hippo can be said to "speak" in a gentle voice is when it is courting. Hippos use a moolike call to get the attention of prospective mates.

4

Ways of the Hippopotamus

"We must suit our behavior to the occasion."
—Cervantes

Because common hippos are so numerous—thousands inhabit Lake George and Lake Edward in central Africa—it has not been difficult for field naturalists to observe their behavior and to record the species' life history. Conversely, researchers have encountered few pygmy hippos in the wild. Not only is *liberiensis* sparsely distributed throughout its range but also it is so shy that one can trek for weeks through its forest habitat and never see a single specimen. Thus most of our knowledge about the pygmy hippo is based on the study of captive animals.

Temperament

Although common hippos are generally peaceable creatures, they are also unpredictable. While *amphibius* will usually retreat or sink beneath the surface when a human approaches, it will attack if it feels threatened. Records kept by African governments reveal that several hundred people are killed by hippopotamuses every year.

The most aggressive hippos are those that have been mal-

The forward-pointing ears of this hippo denote that something has alarmed it. It will probably sink silently below the surface, but it may attack.

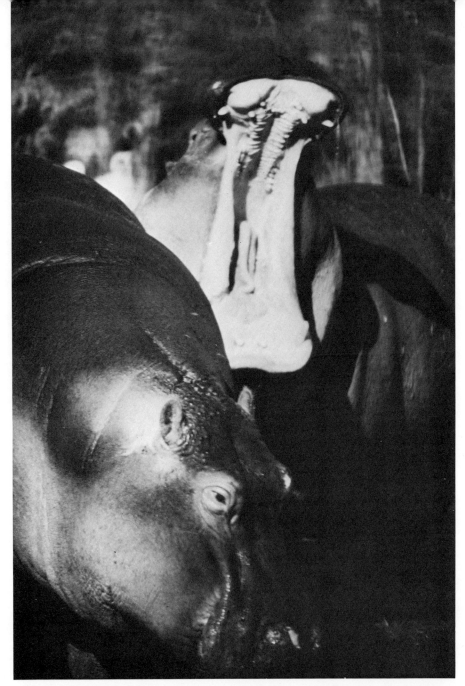

By lowering his head, the hippo on the left acknowledges the dominance of the yawning bull. When making this gesture of submission, bull hippos avoid fights that could result in the death of one of the combatants.

treated by man and old bulls that lead solitary lives. But all mature individuals may attack without provocation. For example, when a grazing hippo encounters a human between itself and the water, the startled beast, thinking its escape route to water is blocked, charges. Cows with small calves are easily infuriated. They are apt to assault boats—including small steamers—that come too close. Canoes are overturned with a toss of the head, and sometimes their passengers are bitten so viciously that they die.

Common hippos are sedentary creatures. As a result, bulls will fight bloody battles to retain possession of the short stretch of shallow water they consider their personal property. A resident hippo and a "claim jumper" do not fight immediately, however. First they open their mouths wide and yawn. If one of them is intimidated by this threat display, he closes his mouth and retreats.

When yawning fails to drive an intruder away, the bull defending his territory rises high out of the water and drops back in, drenching his opponent. The trespasser may still stand his ground. Then, suddenly, the two bulls rush at each other with wide open mouths. Upon contact, they stand parallel, heads facing in opposite directions, and drive their sharp canines into their competitor with sideways blows of their huge heads. Contests between evenly matched bulls can last for hours— from time to time the combatants rest by walking backward a few feet. Then they catch their breath, roar in anger, and return to the fray.

Despite their thick skins, common hippos suffer severe wounds in fights and the skins of old males are "seamed with the scars of war." Territorial battles may end in death. While a fatality can be due to excessive bleeding or the piercing of the heart by a canine, most deaths are the result of strategy on the part of battle-wise bulls. They try to crush one of a rival's forefeet,

Although this hippo bears several scars as the result of territorial battles, they are minor ones. When two battle-wise bulls meet, one of the contestants may be so severely injured that he dies.

which makes it impossible for the animal to stand or walk. As a result, it starves to death.

Female hippos rarely fight. Gregarious, they delight in nestling close together on a sandbar and sleeping. Common hippo cows also practice "togetherness" when in the water. They float with their bodies as near to each other as possible and rest their heads on one another's necks.

Because pygmy hippos are not gregarious—only a single specimen or a cow and a calf are normally seen at one time— zoologists know little of the relationship between members of this species in the wild. Meanwhile, it has been learned in zoos that only a pair of pygmy hippos or a mother and her calf can be

48

confined in the same area. This is because mature bulls will fight as will any related females once they are old enough to mate.

Diet

Both species of hippopotamus are herbivorous. The favorite menu of the pygmy hippo includes succulent plants, tender shoots, roots, various grasses, and fallen fruits. Nocturnal feeders, pygmy hippos follow well-defined paths through underbrush to reach foraging areas. In time, these passageways become vegetation-roofed tunnels.

"Togetherness" in a hippo pool. Common female hippos would rather nestle close than fight, on land or in water. Ever-present birds are busy removing insects and ticks even when the great beasts are floating.

Normally, sunbathing hippos rest their huge and heavy heads on each other's backs. This group is the exception. Note the well-worn pathway at the right of the picture. It leads to the animals' grazing grounds.

Common hippos also have private paths leading to their feeding areas. Eventually, the paths become three-foot-wide walkways cut through riverbanks that may be two hundred feet high. Hippo trails in swampy areas are easy to spot. They consist of two deep ruts made by the feet with a dip in the middle scraped out by the belly.

To warn other hippos that they are on private property, common hippos mark their paths. This is done while defecating by rapidly vibrating the slightly flattened tail and using it as a paddle to scatter the feces as far as possible. While bulls invariably attack members of their species that ignore their "no trespassing signs," females do not distribute their feces and may allow other hippos to pass unchallenged along their paths.

Zoologists have not as yet established whether or not pygmy hippopotamuses mark their territory with excrement. They probably do—in captivity pygmy hippos use the tail to throw their dung against the fence that encloses them.

Although common hippos snack on water plants during the day, they feed mostly at night on land. Each individual has its own pear-shaped grazing territory that extends as much as six miles inland. The size of the "pear" varies with the time

At dusk, hippos leave the safety of the water and come ashore to forage for their food. Each individual hippo eats about 150 pounds of vegetation every night.

of year. It is biggest during the dry season when a hippo may wander as much as twenty miles a night in search of food. After the rainy season when grass is plentiful and lush, the pear is small because then hippos need not venture far from water to forage.

In order to fill their enormous three-chambered stomachs, common hippos have to eat a tremendous amount of grass every day, approximately 150 pounds. Although their diet is high in cellulose—the chief component of the cell walls of plants that is difficult to digest—hippos assimilate it with ease. Special pockets in their stomachs shelter organisms that feed on cellulose and reduce it to a pulp that can be digested without effort.

Amphibius is a close grazer, preferring loosely rooted grasses that can be plucked easily out of the ground. When too many hippos forage in an area, only the strongly rooted species of grass can survive the pressure. However, whenever the hippopotamus population is not too dense, the animal droppings left behind stimulate the growth of grass.

Besides thriving on short and often tough grass, common hippos frequently raid rice paddies, cornfields, orchards, and sugar plantations. During these forays, hippos cause considerable damage. They not only consume a huge amount of food but also trample down crops with the wide soles of their big feet. Some hippos even carry away sugar cane or cornstalks from cultivated fields for "snacks" on the way back to their watering places.

Aquatic Activities

Of all the numerous families of amphibious even-toed ungulates that roamed the Old World in prehistoric times, only the Hippopotamidae has survived to the present day. Because hippos have lived in and near water for untold centuries, they

52

Common hippos are close grazers. Note the white cattle egret, and the tick bird perched on the side of the standing hippo's neck.

should be accomplished swimmers. They are not. Nevertheless, an aroused common hippo "can overtake almost any man-powered boat and even motorboats by paddling like a dog."

Compared to such aquatic animals as otters and seals, hippos perform poorly in water. Yet common hippos feel far more secure when floating than when on land. Similarly, pygmy hippos will rush into water when frightened. They do not have to dash very far—the skins of pygmy hippos dry up quickly and crack if not kept moist, so the animals never venture very far from water.

Field observations have revealed that common hippos spend more than half their lives floating. It has also been established that common hippos prefer slow-moving or stagnant waters about five feet deep. Here, they are not forced to swim but are able to walk.

Common hippos delight in pools carpeted with aquatic plants where they can vanish without leaving a ripple to mark their disappearance. Beside aquatic plants, beds of reeds and overhanging branches conceal floating hippos. Often the animals could not be detected were it not for the egrets and other water birds that perch on their heads. Hippos tolerate them because the birds not only pick ticks from their skins but also remove flies and other irritating insects from wounds, thus preventing infection. Common hippo skins also get "beauty treatments" from *Labeo velifer*, a carplike fish. *Velifer*, known to Africans as the "cattle egret of the water," removes algae and other foreign material from *amphibius'* skin.

Zoologists have studied hippos in hopes of learning what changes take place within their bodies during dives. As a result, we know that while common hippos can stay under water for approximately six minutes, they normally remain submerged only two to four minutes. The amount of carbon dioxide in the bloodstream determines the duration of a dive. When a certain

Hippos prefer shallow waters where they can stand and, by lifting their pillar-like legs, float or swim. Those pictured here are youngsters frolicking.

level of carbon dioxide is reached, a hippo automatically surfaces and exchanges the stale air in its lungs for fresh air.

Experiments with captive hippos have established that the heart rate varies depending on whether *amphibius* is above or below water. During a dive, a common hippo's heart rate drops from ninety beats a minute to only twenty beats! But the most astonishing discovery made during the experiments was that the common hippo can regulate its buoyancy by alternately expanding and compressing the rib cage and diaphragm.

Because hippos are able to make themselves heavier or lighter by inhaling and exhaling, they not only can rise and sink in the water at will but also move swiftly along the bottom. Watching hippos run or walk under water is a thrilling sight but, until recently, only professional diver-photographers had witnessed it. Now the construction of a unique underwater viewing tank at Mizma Springs in Kenya makes it possible for any visitor to have the experience.

During the dry season, common hippos frequently travel considerable distances seeking water. As a result, they are found in mountain streams eight thousand feet above sea level, in brackish waters swimming from one coastal estuary to another, and in the ocean several miles off the East African coast.

There is no way of telling if the longest recorded journey made by a hippopotamus was to find water. But the trek of a hippo affectionately known to South Africans as Huberta is well documented. In 1928, Huberta left St. Lucia Bay in Zululand and started southward. Her progress was reported in newspapers that detailed what the wandering hippo ate, where she bathed, and how many miles she covered each day. Huberta became a national pet, and a law was passed protecting her. But when she reached Cape Province in April, 1931, after a trek of a thousand miles, she was shot by an irate farmer whose crops had been trampled. When the authorities examined Huberta's body, they discovered that "she" was a male!

Social Organization

As indicated, little is known of the relationships of pygmy hippos in the wild. On the other hand, zoologists have long been aware that common hippos follow a behavior pattern

Common hippo herd basking on a sandbar near hippo pool. Note the young hippos amidst the adults.

that enables them to live in communities composed of from twenty to one hundred individuals.

When the social organization of the common hippo was first investigated, naturalists wrongly believed that each community was directed by a dominant male. Now we know that it is the mature females in a herd, acting as a group, that govern a hippo community. Thus it is the females that decide where a herd's territory should be established. If possible, they choose a sandbar in the middle of a river because such sites enable the herd to vanish quickly beneath the water when danger threatens. If a sandbar is not available, the females settle down on a bank.

Both large and small herds divide their territories in the same

Common hippos have rules to be followed about who stands and who lies down in a crèche.

fashion. In the center is an area known as a crèche, which is occupied by females and their young. The crèche is ringed with refuges—the individual territories of adult bulls. The nearer a refuge is to the perimeter of a crèche, the greater the chance that its inhabitant will be able to mate with one of the females. This is why hippo bulls constantly wage territorial battles.

When male hippos are approximately a year old, they leave their mothers and the safety of the crèche to claim territories well beyond those of their elders. Then, as these youngsters mature, they fight their way into the inner circle of refuges.

Sometimes juveniles are harassed by adult bulls even though they stay far away from the older males' territories. When this happens, the persecuted immature bulls may flee back to the crèche, where the females band together and protect them.

Although male and female hippos frequently pay "social calls" on one another, the most powerful bull in a herd would not dare enter a crèche without permission. Moreover, while in a crèche, a male must obey certain rules. For example, if one of the females stands up, the bull is required to lie down immediately and not rise until the female lies down again. If this is not done, all the adult females in the crèche will attack the visitor and drive him away.

Raising a Family

There is nothing shy about a common hippo cow during the breeding season. While, as noted, a female may utter moolike calls to attract the attention of bulls, she chooses her suitor by boldly entering his refuge. Mating takes place in the water.

Usually, common hippos in the wild breed at the end of the dry season. Approximately eight months later—the time of greatest precipitation—the young are born. This reproductive cycle insures that the females will have sufficient grass to eat and thus be able to produce the milk needed to feed the calves.

When a cow is about to give birth, she leaves the herd and goes to a secluded spot where she feels secure. Often females choose to have their babies in the water. A hippo born under water learns to swim before it can walk—it must rise quickly to the surface to take its first breath. After filling its lungs, the infant dives and begins to suckle, a process repeated thousands of times during the twelve-month nursing period.

At birth, common hippo calves are about three feet long, eighteen inches tall, and weigh between sixty and a hundred

Although anatomically correct, this early engraving of a hippo cow and her calf gives the wrong impression. Normally, baby hippos feed under water, rising repeatedly to the surface for a gulp of air.

pounds. When five minutes old, they not only can swim but also run and walk. However, several weeks pass before the calf is taken to the crèche and introduced to its "aunts"—females who babysit infant hippos while their mothers are away. Once in the crèche, the newcomer seeks out members of the same sex and plays with them. The females join in a form of hide-and-seek and roll over in the water with stiff legs. Males have special games too, but their favorite sport is engaging in mock battles.

Common hippos are devoted parents. They are also very strict disciplinarians. As soon as a calf is able to follow its mother for long distances, the two take frequent hikes over rough ground. During these excursions, the baby is taught to stay close to one of its mother's shoulders. The youngster also quickly discovers that it must copy its mother: if she runs, stops suddenly, or turns around, the infant must do the same.

If a baby is slow to learn or refuses to obey, it is severely punished. Its mother may lash the disobedient pupil with her

Common hippo young are miniature copies of their parents. Note the toes on this zoo baby.

head, roll the youngster over and over, or even slash him with her tusks. This treatment continues until the young hippo cowers in submission. Then the mother licks and caresses it.

When babies are threatened by predators or ill-tempered bulls, the mothers stand between offspring and the potential attacker. Whenever a female fears that harm may befall her calf as the two pass a certain place, she makes sure that she is the one who swims or walks nearest the source of possible danger. If a floating cow feels secure, she does not object if her calf clambers up on her broad back and uses it as a raft.

Baby hippos do ride on their mothers' backs, but the one shown here is much too big to be carried. The artist shows a hippo "blowing" like a whale. Actually, hippos expel water from their nostrils in a fine spray.

Pygmy hippos breed freely in captivity, which insures the survival of the species. Note the piglike appearance of the baby.

Practically nothing is known of how pygmy hippos in the wild choose mates and raise young. However, by observing *liberiensis* in captivity, we have learned that in this species courtship originates with the bull. To show his affection, a male lays his head on the back of the female, who usually runs away three or four times before accepting him.

Pygmy hippo babies—which weigh between six and ten pounds—are born about seven months after their parents mate. In zoos, pygmy cows are not allowed to give birth in the water because their calves are apt to drown. Unlike their larger cousins, pygmy hippo infants neither swim nor dive instinctively but must be taught these skills. Until they have mastered them, the babies are nursed on land.

Although the young only suckle two or three times a day, they consume a tremendous amount of milk. As a result, their growth is extremely rapid. When five months old, a baby pygmy hippo weighs ten times as much as it did at birth.

5

Conservation

"Let tomorrow be as today."
—Anon.

Several different predators prey on the hippopotamus. When young hippos become independent of their mothers, hyenas and wild dogs attack them. Crocodiles also snatch baby hippos, but it is doubtful that they eat as many of them as tradition maintains. Both lions and leopards pounce on immature hippos and, occasionally, a pride of hungry lions attempts to kill an adult. Usually, the attempt is a failure and the intended victim not only saves its own life but also severely injures some of the lions.

Hippos can protect their offspring from four-footed predators and defend themselves from lions but they are unable to cope with their most dangerous enemy, man. From ancient times to the present day, humans have killed hippos for food and for sport.

As indicated, hippos were originally hunted for meat, skins, and ivory. But Africans, when they began to farm, destroyed hippos for raiding their fields. Hippos were considered a nuisance in ancient Egypt and they were listed as one of the

2.

3.

4.

Hippopot. in gemma.

Hippopotamus Herculanensis.

Hippopot. Gorii.

Published in 1789, Petri Artedi's Disputatio de Veterum Scriptorum Hippopotomo *presents—with the author's comments—all known ancient writings about the hippopotamus. Not only is Artedi's work valuable for its text but also for its three sets of illustrations, most of which had not previously appeared in print. Those shown here are from the third set.*

"miseries of agriculture" in a papyrus dealing with farming.

Three ways to slay hippos with primitive weapons were developed centuries ago. One was to dig a pit and line it with sharp stakes capable of piercing a hippo's vital organs when it fell on them. In the second technique, ingeniously fashioned traps were hung from trees lining hippo paths. The third method was employed only by brave men. Hunting hippos from small boats with harpoons and spears is a most dangerous undertaking.

The ancient Egyptians not only were daring but also were extremely skilled hippopotamus hunters. According to Diodorus, a Greek historian who visited Egypt between 60 and 57 B.C.,

67

Old print depicts a spear trap suspended in a tree above a hippopotamus path.

When hunting hippos, Betoana tribesmen in South Africa boldly jumped into the water armed with snares and spears to make a kill, after pursuing their quarry in boats.

a band of hunters armed with spears to which ropes were attached would chase a hippopotamus in boats, "and closing in on all sides would wound it." When the animal tried to escape, the hunters would play out the rope until the beast's strength "failed from lack of blood."

Although arrow, harpoon, and spear exterminated most of the hippos that lived along the upper reaches of the Nile at a very early date, the populations of common hippos elsewhere in Africa withstood human pressure until the coming of the

Europeans. No one knows how many thousands of common hippos were destroyed between the middle and the end of the nineteenth century. But the toll taken by those who "felt challenged by the mere sight of these giants to try their firearms on them" was enormous.

Today, tractors pose a greater threat to the hippopotamus than poachers' snares or sportsmen's guns. As the world's ever-growing population demands more and more food, much of the common hippo's traditional habitat is being transformed into farmland.

Because of the tendency of hippos to feast on cultivated crops when available, most farmers are convinced they would be much better off if there were no hippos nearby. For example, in Gambia on Africa's northwest coast where rice has been an important crop for nearly three hundred years, the government is constantly urged to kill hippos. While official investigations have established that hippos do raid rice paddies, it has been learned that the damage they do is greatly exaggerated. Actually, baboons, bush pigs, and weaverbirds do as much harm. But complaints are not lodged against them because, when a government hunter shoots a hippopotamus, its flesh, which is considered a delicacy, is given to local farmers.

Hippos that prefer farm products to wild grasses need not be shot. Wildlife experts have discovered that fences two or three feet high will keep hippos out of fields. The fences can be flimsy —the animals do not realize that they are capable of breaking through even a sturdily constructed barrier.

However, the wholesale felling of trees for fencing can cause the deforestation of sparsely wooded areas. When this happens, the cleared land is apt to be used for cattle raising. As rural Africans are inclined to measure an individual's wealth by the number of cattle he owns, there is a great danger of overgrazing. Then, as the grass cover vanishes, the soil erodes. The

A typical African scene during the dry season. The lake in which the wildebeest are wading is shrinking, which will not only make it more difficult for the white pelicans to find food but also will reduce the level of water in the hippo pool (foreground). Note the white bird on the back of the hippo leaving the water.

resulting economic loss is far greater than that due to the activities of marauding hippos.

Obviously, controlling Africa's free-roaming hippos poses serious problems to conservationists. Equally difficult is the proper management of the hippos confined to national parks and wildlife reserves. Hardy, long lived, and resistant to disease, hippos prosper when protected, despite predators' attacks and droughts that dry up their pools and wallows. As a result, the hippopotamus population in parks and refuges increases and overcrowding occurs.

When a habitat can no longer support the number of hippos

71

that range through it, a difficult decision must be made. Should some of the hippos be "cropped" (killed) in order to keep their numbers and the available habitat in balance? Or should the animals be left alone and natural controls be trusted to keep the the hippo population in check?

Authorities disagree as to the best approach. Some favor the "kill them to save them" technique. Others advocate the "leave them alone" method. The difficulty is that both procedures have merit. Cropping was very successful in Uganda, where thousands of hippos were stripping the savannah of grass, not only depleting their food supply but also forcing other grass-eating animals to migrate. After some six thousand hippos were killed, the overgrazed areas recovered and many species returned to the region.

All the hippos cropped in Uganda were examined and much information was collected and analyzed. At the same time, the possibility of utilizing hippos as a food source was also explored. The report of this investigation states that " . . . the exceptionally high protein content makes hippopotamus meat an extremely valuable food item." The tribesmen who feasted on the carcasses of the cropped hippos after they were dissected did not need to be told about hippo meat—until laws were passed protecting the hippopotamus, it was a staple in the diet of African peoples living beside bodies of water.

Because high protein food is sorely lacking in Africa, the cropping of surplus hippos could help meet a serious nutritional need. However, as zoologists Hans Fradrich and Ernst Lang point out, national parks should not be considered sources of a regular meat supply. Instead, hippopotamus farms should be established and the animals, like pigs, be "bred, raised, and butchered on demand."

Incidentally, the hippopotamus is not only a potential source of meat but also it is presently responsible for a thriving fishing

Young common hippo displays yawning technique for bored mother. The excrement of hippos fertilizes aquatic plants on which fish feed.

industry. The tremendous amount of rich, organic material in the form of excrement that hippos deposit in water stimulates the growth of the microscopic plants on which fish feed. In Uganda's Lake George—home of thousands of hippos—nearly seven million pounds of fish are caught every year. Were it not for the lake's hippos, fisherman's nets would not be so full.

A number of scientists are convinced that far fewer hippos could supply Lake George's aquatic vegetation with ample fertilizer and feel that the lake's huge population of hippos should be cropped regularly. These authorities contend that if the number of hippos were controlled, the dangers of overgrazing would be eliminated, thus insuring that both hippos and other species of grass-eating animals native to the region would have sufficient food.

Other scientists insist that any cropping of hippos is unnecessary. These individuals support their conviction by describing what has happened in Zaire where the hippopotamus is free of human interference. The unavailability of water during droughts, the lack of food, the pressure of predators, and the tendency of hippos to produce less young when crowded have acted as natural controls. As a result, the hippo population in Zaire has remained relatively stable.

Actually, the managers of Zaire's conservation program have been extremely fortunate. Normally, it takes decades for natural population control to be effective. Meanwhile, the countryside could be devastated by herds of hungry hippos expanding their range in search of food.

If you were in charge of conserving Africa's wildlife, how would you handle the problem of the hippopotamus? Obviously, one of your first tasks would be to organize expeditions to take a census of pygmy hippos in the wild and to observe their behavior. Even if these investigations should reveal that the

Although comparatively rare in the wild, pygmy hippos thrive in captivity. Thus there is no danger that this species will be exterminated as a result of the destruction of its habitat by man.

species is endangered, you would be able to announce that the species is in no danger of becoming extinct—*liberiensis* breeds freely in captivity.

While supervising field studies of the pygmy hippo, you would also have to decide how to control its huge relation. Should surplus animals be cropped or should nature be allowed to take its course? This is not an easy question to answer. The future of the hippopotamus in the wild is bleak unless proper control methods are employed.

The most difficult task in devising a program to preserve the hippopotamus is determining whether or not cropping is cruel.

Here's a happy hippo! It has discovered the possibility of taking a nap, basking in the sun, and enjoying a mud bath all at the same time.

The chances are, after weighing all the facts, you'd conclude that killing some hippos so that others may live is a practical procedure. Otherwise, there is no guarantee that future generations will be able to see hippos floating lethargically in placid pools or basking on sandbars in Africa's muddy rivers.

Index